Trees and Deforestation

COLOURED VERSION

CHILDREN SAVING OUR PLANET SERIES

CAROL SUTTERS

Illustrated by William Fong

AuthorHouse™ UK
1663 Liberty Drive
Bloomington, IN 47403 USA
www.authorhouse.co.uk
UK TFN: 0800 0148641 (Toll Free inside the UK)
UK Local: 02036 956322 (+44 20 3695 6322 from outside the UK)

Because of the dynamic nature of the Internet, any web addresses or links contained in this book may have changed since publication and may no longer be valid. The views expressed in this work are solely those of the author and do not necessarily reflect the views of the publisher, and the publisher hereby disclaims any responsibility for them.

Any people depicted in stock imagery provided by Getty Images are models, and such images are being used for illustrative purposes only.
Certain stock imagery © Getty Images.

This book is printed on acid-free paper.

ISBN: 978-1-6655-8791-4 (sc)
978-1-6655-8792-1 (e)

Library of Congress Control Number: 2021907198

Print information available on the last page.

Published by AuthorHouse 04/07/2021

authorHOUSE®

Mum *says, "Today we shall go to a nearby wood for a walk to talk about the importance of trees. It is important we respect trees and understand how they help to preserve the planet."*

Sapliings

"Trees take many years to grow. They serve a very important role in the balance in woods with other animals and plants known as the local microenvironment. This is sometimes also called an ecosystem. Trees are important for our climate and our survival."

"From a little sapling, a big tree grows."

Ground

Soil

Roots

"The roots grow into the soil and absorb water and nutrients which make the branches grow and eventually the leaves grow. As the tree grows, the bark gets woody and thicker."

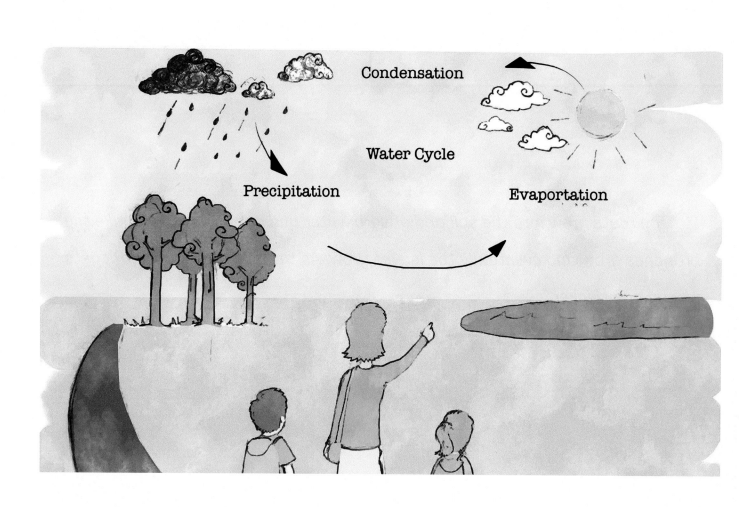

"The trees also play an important part in the water cycle as the roots absorb water and take it up to the leaves where it evaporates and goes into the air as water vapour. The green leaves are also very important in removing carbon dioxide from the air and producing oxygen for us to breathe."

"The tree trunk is also very important as it gets thicker and woody."

"We use wood from trees for making furniture, building houses and boats, but also for making paper on which we write or use for other purposes such as toilet paper."

"We also burn wood and this can cause pollution."

"Toilet paper use was first introduced by Chinese people as it helped with toilet cleanliness."

" It is estimated a single tree can make 1,500 rolls of toilet paper. Because of the huge and growing toilet paper use around the world, a large number of trees have been cut down to produce toilet paper."

"The rapid rate of deforestation, as it is called, has had a significant impact on the global climate patterns as it leads to a reduction in the amount of rainfall in some areas. It also reduces carbon dioxide capture and oxygen production."

"Deforestation also destroys the natural habitat of many plants and animals and this can be harmful to humans in the long term."

"What can we do to reduce the negative effect?", says Tom.

Mum replies, *"The toilet paper industry is trying to use recovered fibres, that is recycled fibres so that we reuse paper material and not just throw it away."*

"Can the factories use less fossil fuels?", asks Kate?

"Yes", says Mum.

"The factories use less carbon fuels for their energy in making the paper so that they produce less carbon emissions, cause less pollution and environmental warming."

"What can we do to use less toilet paper or reduce the pollution?", asks Tom.

Mum says "We can try and buy toilet paper that has been made from recycled materials.

This is usually shown on the package."

"We should do this next time at the Supermarket", says Tom.

"Can we reduce paper waste in other ways?", asks Kate.

"Yes", Mum says.

"There has been a big attempt in offices and homes to try and go paperless or just to reduce the amount of waste paper we produce. Many official documents and books are sent via electronic means which means it is not produced as a paper copy. Fewer people buy a daily newspaper, instead they read news on computers, phones or watch television. Also lots of advertising and messaging is done electronically via mobile phones and computers which cuts down the amount of postal mail we send and receive. Sending fewer letters by the post office transport reduces the use of fossil fuels in the form of petrol and this also avoids pollution."

What did we learn today? (tick the box if you understood and agree)

☐ Trees are important in they are part of the water cycle and take water from the earth through their trunks and release it into the air.

☐ The leaves on trees also help to remove carbon from the air in the form of carbon dioxide and they produce oxygen. This counteracts carbon pollution by humans.

☐ We must take care not to cut down too many trees for wood, paper and furniture as they take many, many years to grow again.

☐ We cannot compensate the rate at which we are cutting down trees by planting new trees so we are destroying these precious forests.

Find out about Kate and Tom's neighbourhood houses in book 5.

Children Saving our Planet Series

Books

1. **Tom and Kate Go to Westminster CHILDREN'S REVOLT**

2. **Kate and Tom Learn About Fossil Fuels**

3. **Tom and Kate Chose Green Carbon**

4. **Tress and Deforestation**

5. **Our Neighbourhood Houses**

6. **Our Neighbourhood Roads**

7. **Shopping at the Farm Shop**

8. **Travelling to a Holiday by the Sea**

9. **Picnic at the Seaside on Holiday**

These series of simple books explain the landmark importance of Children's participation in the Extinction rebellion protest. Children actively want to encourage and support adults to urgently tackle both the Climate and the Biodiversity emergencies. The booklets enable children at an early age to understand some of the scientific principles that are affecting the destruction of the planet. If global political and economic systems fail to address the climate emergency, the responsibility will rest upon children to save the Planet for themselves.

This series is dedicated to

Theodore, Aria and Ophelia

Printed in the United States
by Baker & Taylor Publisher Services